AFFIRMATIONS AND THOUGHT FORMS

You Can Change Your Mind!

A Discourse from the

Ascended Master ST. GERMAIN

Linda Stein-Luthke
Martin F. Luthke, Ph.D.

Expansion Publishing

AFFIRMATIONS AND THOUGHT FORMS

You Can Change Your Mind!

A Discourse from the Ascended Master ST. GERMAIN

Linda Stein-Luthke
Martin F. Luthke, Ph.D.

Copyright 1997 by Linda Stein-Luthke & Martin F. Luthke

Fourth printing: May 2007

ISBN 978-0-9656927-1-X

Published by

Expansion Publishing
P.O. Box 516 - Chagrin Falls, OH 44022
USA

Contents

Foreword

It is with great joy that we offer this second booklet in a series of publications on applied metaphysics. Since it is often easier to relate to new information if you have at least a vague idea of the person or source it is coming from, we wish to introduce ourselves in a few sentences.

Linda Stein-Luthke is the one who actually brought the following text to paper, but she is not the one who composed it. Among her many gifts is the ability to "channel" wisdom from sources other than her human consciousness. Channeling is a process during which we open ourselves to higher-vibrational frequencies of Light. The frequencies we access can be from our own being or from other beings of Light working in conjunction with us. For many years Linda has been channeling highly evolved spiritual beings of Light, most frequently the Ascended Masters El Morya Khan and St. Germain. The latter is the true author of this publication.

Linda is or has been a mother and foster mother, successful business woman, activist and philanthropist in the women's community, a teacher of astrology and Applied Metaphysics, and, first and foremost, a seeker throughout her life. She has traveled to India, Nepal, and Cyprus and has studied and channeled with Masters there and in the United States. Her training has been within the Hindu, Buddhist, Sufi, Christian, and Jewish traditions.

Linda, or "Leia," as she is called by the Masters, is working as a metaphysical teacher and healer with individuals and groups, utilizing the various skills she has learned in many years "on the path." Linda has authored several books in collaboration with the Ascended Masters (see appendix).

Dr. Martin Luthke is a clinical psychologist, author, teacher of Applied Metaphysics, and energy-based healer. A *Diplomate, Comprehensive Energy Psychology*, he is the founder and director of the *Institute of Psychoenergetic Healing*. The Masters refer to Martin by his spirit name, "Manalus." He took responsibility for the editing and production aspects of this collaborative project.[1]

In addition to their work, Linda and Martin are enjoying their two adult and two young children, one grandchild, and four companion animals.

St. Germain is probably the best known of the Ascended Masters, a group of Light Beings who once walked this Earth in human bodies and who have gained complete awareness of their Totality. They are serving humanity and all of Creation from the higher planes of existence, offering their light, love, and wisdom freely to all at this time of accelerating change and awakening.

While it may be more than a stretch for some to accept the reality of invisible Light Beings in general and Ascended Masters in particular, we can only appeal to your willingness to suspend your disbelief and to entertain, and

---

[1] We thank Julianne Stein and Katherine Hvistendahl for their help in the editing process of this publication.

2

test, the teachings offered on these pages. The authors of this publication as well as countless other perfectly "normal" and "sane" human beings have opened themselves to an awareness of the reality of Light Beings, and have benefited immeasurably in the process.

Most importantly, however, listen to your own "still small voice within" and to the guidance you will be receiving, if only you choose to sit, meditate, and ask. We offer our truth as a service, but we wish you to honor your own truth, above all. And now, enjoy the journey within.

Love and Light,

May, 2007   Linda & Martin

Introduction

After the success of our first publication, *Balancing the Light Within,* a channeled discourse on healing from the Ascended Master St. Germain, the question arose as to what would be the most effective way to utilize the information received in that publication. Of course, the Master had an answer, which resulted in this new manual. Our goal with these short, concise books is to explain as simply as possible the metaphysical laws of manifestation. To some that may seem an impossible task, but as we repeatedly hear in these channeling sessions, the truth is simple. It is the human mind that chooses to complicate matters. And once that mind is trained to think in new and positive ways, the concept of manifestation becomes easily accessible.

We have also been hearing repeatedly that the energies that create manifestation are more powerful than ever before. Because the vibrational frequencies of the Earth plane are rising more rapidly every day (and this is being observed by scientists), the energies that create manifestation are more easily available to us. As we grow in wisdom and awareness, we become capable, then, of utilizing these powerful vibrational frequencies to create healing and transformation within.

In *Balancing the Light Within,* the basic goal was to explain how the Light can be utilized to create healing and well-being. In the present publication information is being shared that takes that process one step further. By directly addressing patterns of thinking, even more efficient and healthy ways of living can be created. We hope you will find this publication both enjoyable and useful in its applications.

Love and Light,

Linda & Martin

Chapter 1

Why We Wish to Share With You
Once Again

We thank you, beloved friend, for your willingness once again to let us, so to speak, write through you so that others may read these words. We understand this has been an intense time of change and growth upon the human plane for all beings, and we wish to extend our help to you as you traverse this new, uncharted path for all of humanity.

We are here to help you. We are beings of Light who have also been human in many, many embodiments, but at this time are choosing to remain in a higher-vibrational frequency in order to be of service to all who dwell on Earth while the planet moves into a new time and space that has never been witnessed by any living creature at any time. It is an exciting time to be alive on the planet you call Earth, and it is also a time of very rapid and, at times, for the human mind, confusing change. And so, we are here to be of help in any way we can. The one we call Leia, who has agreed to allow us to work with her, is a being who, after much encouragement from us, has tried all the information she will share with you here in collaboration with her partner Manalus. Together they have walked the path of truth and have found that the simple metaphysical laws we have shared with them have proven effective when utilized with diligence and purity of heart.

It is not easy to be human now. It never was. For the Earth plane has been a plane of free will, and once one has manifested into that frequency, what occurs for many is a forgetting of the very laws of manifestation that brought one to the Earth in the first place. And so, for all of you who read this publication it is a journey into remembering what you have always known, but have chosen until now to forget. You chose to forget so that you could test living on the Earth more fully, or so you thought.

What you have probably found up to this point is that the Earth can be very confusing if one lives by the laws that are prevalent in human thinking today. These laws we call the *Laws of Manipulation and Self-Gratification*. They are not the same as the *Metaphysical Laws of Manifestation*, but they do operate from the same universal principles: That you will reap what you have sown. This is also what many humans have called *Karmic Law*.

All of these laws can appear to be incomprehensible and difficult -- not worth the effort to comprehend. But when one has suffered enough from not choosing to know these universal truths, then one may finally stop and listen. This is what happened for Leia and Manalus. And this is what is now happening for many others as well.

We, of the Ascended Master realm, can watch but *cannot help unless asked*, because you live on a plane of free will. But when we are asked, our help is without reservation. Our function is to empower you through knowledge in how to make new free choices that can end the suffering and create healing and greater harmony for the Earth as it travels to a new life and Golden Era for all. So, thank you for choosing to take this journey with us, even if it is just for a little while. We promise you, it will be fascinating and fruitful, if you allow it.

Chapter 2

The Principles of Manifestation

For the sake of brevity, and because the human mind cannot comprehend completely why these laws work, for this endeavor we shall simply state the *Laws of Manifestation* as they apply to the Earth plane at this time.

All of creation is vibration. This is most important to remember. All creation, everything that you can see, and everything you cannot see, operates on a vibrational frequency of sound and Light. As one develops what is called psychic abilities, one can begin to experience a greater variety of the vibrational frequencies, and utilize that experience for greater awareness. But even without these abilities one can still know simply from experiences on the Earth that all is vibration. Your scientists know this and utilize this information in order to create. It is the same for you, also. You just may not, until this moment, have understood that this is so.

Consider, for instance, the atom, the building block of all that you behold with your physical senses. Every atom has movement within its structure. That movement occurs at a certain frequency, depending on the structure of the atom. You cannot see the atom with your eye, yet you can see what a group of atoms can become. The same is true for all the different vibrational frequencies. You may not see them or sense them with your five senses, but you are always experiencing what is being created by these frequencies. This brings us to the next principle or law.

All manifestation begins as higher-vibrational frequencies. Again, you may not consciously be aware that this is so. But it simply is so. Everything that you behold with your conscious five senses was first in existence on a higher-vibrational field of energy. In fact, all creation exists simultaneously in these higher-vibrational fields. On Earth, they manifest into what you call time and space. These are Earth-bound concepts: time and space. Outside the confines of your planet these concepts are not applicable. And so, all that has been created, or will ever be created for your planet, exists *now* simply to be pulled into the Earth and utilized when your space and time are right for it to manifest.

There are many possible realities that exist at higher frequency waiting to become probable realities, and then to become human experience. Now, this can become complicated for the human mind to comprehend, but again, for the sake of brevity, we simply ask you to consider that there are many options available in the timeless-spaceless higher-vibrational frequencies, and the human can have free will as to which reality the being wishes to experience on Earth. We say *can* have free will, but indeed *does* have free will whether the being is aware of it or not. The purpose of this publication is to aid the human in becoming aware of this choice, and then activating these principles for the Highest Good.

All thought exists first at higher-vibrational frequencies and then can create and manifest into physical reality. You see this every day in every way. Now we ask you to become aware of this simple truth. Before you do anything,

10

make any move, build or create anything on the human plane, you first experience the thought of this. *Without the thought, there is no creation.* Because of lack of discipline, you may not be aware of all the thoughts that go into creating everything that you experience, and, indeed, you very often may choose to credit outside influences for much that you experience, but we tell you now, and we will tell you again as this publication continues, it is *you* creating, through your thoughts -- whether you are consciously aware of it or not -- all that occurs for you at any time. You choose your experience from the thoughts.

Thoughts begin first as possible realities, then as probable realities, and finally as manifestation. And so, you may entertain an idea of traveling to visit your aunt in another place. You have the thought of it. You check all the factors that would make such a journey possible, and realize that it is possible. Then you proceed to plan it, making it a probability. And once all of the plans are in place, you travel to your aunt for a visit. The visit has manifested into physical reality. All manifestation follows an identical pattern.

Once a thought is created, as with all creation, it exists forever as an energy pattern, or vibrational frequency. The only change possible is from one vibrational frequency to another. But it will always exist. Your scientists know that all creation is eternal. And, indeed, outside the time-space continuum, it *all exists simultaneously*. The scientists also know that even though all perceived creation exists eternally, it is possible to have whatever has been created change form. So, you have created a physical thing that has outlived its usefulness -- perhaps it is now a pile of trash. What can you do with it? In many cases, you seek to destroy it by fire. But even then, look after the flames have died and see what has happened. There are still ashes to contend with. Nothing ever simply disappears, it only changes form.

All of creation is subject to Karmic Law. The basic law of Karma, for the sake of brevity and ease of comprehension, is that you reap what you have sown. When one asks, as one often does, "Why me?", this can be the answer one may accept. It is not a heartless answer. It is simply the law of manifestation least likely to be accepted and most constantly utilized by all humans.

There is hope, however, for all Karmic Law is subject to change, as is all of creation. Indeed, *all creation is in a constant state of change.* This can be the most confusing statement of all. For we are stating that all creation and manifestation is subject to Karmic Law, and then we tell you your Karma can be changed, and in an instant! Most of humanity, however, is not even aware that Karmic Law exists, making it impossible for them to then understand that it can be changed, once understood. But that is what this publication is, ultimately, all about -- creating change through the positive use of Thought Forms and Affirmations.

Now that you have a grasp of the basic principles, let us begin. Remember, always, that all these words matter little. What will really help you to comprehend what we have said here is *experience.* As we share how to create these changes within yourself and your world, understand that only through applying the information that we offer will you really know that all that has been stated here is real and true. Once applied and experienced, you will then have the

12

comprehension to continue on to even greater awareness of how to exist in full empowerment upon the human plane.

Chapter 3

What are Thought Forms?

Now, we have discussed with you the very bare bones of the Principles of Manifestation, and have stated in them two concepts: Thought Forms and Affirmations. As this is the actual title of this publication, you are probably quite right in wondering what these terms actually mean.

Thought forms are what you are continually thinking, whether you are aware of it or not. Every day, there is a running commentary occurring in your mind that sometimes correlates to what is occurring in your life, and other times is merely the hum of the conscious mind whirring in the background of your life. Every thought becomes a form -- an energy form. Depending on the caliber of the thought, it will assume a certain vibrational frequency that actually creates the form. Now, beings with developed psychic abilities can actually see some of these forms as they are being created, and/or attached to the auric field (energy field) of the individual creating them. Yes, your thoughts, unless otherwise dealt with, will become attached to you and be part of your auric field, the energy field that permeates and surrounds every being upon the planet.

So, what we are saying is that every thought you think contributes to the energetic field surrounding and permeating your physical body. And what we also say is that on some level, you know what this auric field, or energy field is composed of, and *so does everyone around you.* You have all said, at one time or another, I really like to be with that person, she or he is nice to be with, or I don't like to be around that person because it is not comfortable. That is your psychic sensitivity responding to the auric field of another.

You also are aware that some days are good days, and you feel fine, and other days you do not feel quite as well. At different times of a day, depending on many variables, you will "feel" differently with no apparent reason for the change. But the energy field that permeates and encompasses you is sending you signals, vibrational signals, and this is, indeed, what you are responding to.

Suffice it to say, very simply, *you are what you think.* Every aspect of your physical body will respond to what is issuing from your thoughts, and what is affecting you from the thoughts around you. Your scientists are discovering the mind-body connection even as we write these words to you. You can find much literature from your scientific community now to corroborate what we are telling you. So we will not belabor the point. We simply wish you to understand as thoroughly as possible that every thought you have affects you more profoundly than your conscious mind can imagine.

It is therefore most important to understand that you are what you think so that you can then begin to apply the tools we will offer you to create with your thinking that which will transform and heal you, if this is your wish and desire. It can be done with diligence and vigilance.

Most importantly, there must be a desire to be of service to self and others for the *Highest Good of All.* This process is subject to *Cosmic Law* and *Karmic Law*, so if you wish to change yourself in order to harm another, remember you will reap what you sow. That would be your free will. If you wish to use these tools to serve the best interests of self and others, that also, you will reap. Remember this as you investigate your motivations for utilizing what you are learning here.

This investigation will involve the scrupulous investigation of all that you think, and why. First, one must learn the thought forms that are prevalent before one can know how to transform them to create healing and transformation in oneself. So, beloved friend, what are you thinking? Let us investigate.

We start at the beginning, and the beginning is: How do you see yourself now? Who are you that you see and corroborate with certain thought patterns? Are you old, young, pretty, ugly, healthy, weak, strong, fertile, infertile, lonely, angry, happy, sad, kind, mean, generous, greedy, inconsiderate, very considerate, smart, stupid, lazy, industrious, brilliant, wealthy, poor? And so on.

You see, the list is endless, beloved one. You have thought forms about yourself that have literally created who you are at this time in your life. Now you will say, "But no, Masters, I am old, I am sick, I have never been pretty, I do not have any money, so I'm obviously poor, how can you say that the obvious are just thought forms that have created me, when any fool can see that this is simply who I am?" And you will add, "Also, my mother died from heart failure, and that is absolutely how I know I will die also, and very soon. Every one in my family dies young. That is just a fact." And so you

16

shall, beloved friend, if that is what you believe with all your heart will happen to you. We do not say this to be unkind, merely to let you see how the thoughts you have been raised with in this time and space have affected you.

There are also, beloved one, the thoughts of everyone in your time and space field that are affecting you as well. These are the collective thoughts of your environment. That is where it is decided if you are pretty or ugly, if you are young or old, rich or poor, smart or stupid -- and many, many other thoughts which are in the collective mind that you then accept as your own because it is the easiest or most sensible thing to do. It is the "common sense," the thoughts that have been collectively defined by the society in which you choose to live, that decides then how you will perceive yourself. So, are you all the things that society deems you should be in order to be good, beautiful, brilliant, healthy, and wealthy? We doubt it. Those are simply standards that your society holds. No one fulfills the standards, and yet everyone usually decides that because they do not, then they are deficient -- at least in one area or another. It can be an insidious process to hold oneself to what society deems is perfection.

We ask you now to consider that an alternative way of thinking could be more useful and healing for you. In fact, it may allow you to return to health, sanity, and a joy of living you only imagined might be possible for you.

Let it go, beloved child. Let go of the need to be what others think you should be or what you think you should be somewhere in your mind. We ask you to release these thought forms for healing. It is time, dear one, to find a new way of being. Let us help you, if we may.

Chapter 4

Transforming and Releasing Thought Forms

Now, before we begin to address the topic listed at the top of this page, we would first wish to emphasize that not all thought forms need to be transformed and released. This should be quite obvious. If your thought form enhances your well-being without serving ego gratification, then it is a thought to continue carrying as part of your auric field.

Exactly what do we mean by this? You may be questioning the introduction of the term "ego gratification" here. And that would be quite justified. So, we shall clarify. Let us say you are a being who enjoys exercising. It creates a sense of well-being when you take the time and space to do this. You have a thought form in your mind that allows you to enjoy this sense of well-being. Something such as, "When I exercise, I feel healthy and strong. It contributes to my well-being." This is what we would call a positive statement, or affirmation. We will dwell in greater depth upon this concept at a later time. But suffice it to say, this is a useful thought form that will indeed lead to your well-being.

However, suppose you add another thought form into this concept of exercise. And this thought form would be such as, "I am better than the other people I know because I choose to exercise," or "I am better at exercising than the people I see around me." And this thought also gives you a happy feeling. What has happened here is that you are no longer focused on your well-being because you are exercising. Now you are focused on how you perceive yourself in relation to others. Another thought form would be, "I'll show them that I can exercise and take care of myself." As soon as the focus shifts from doing or being for the sake of your own well-being to how you perceive yourself in comparison to others, or how you wish others to perceive you, the thought form now becomes driven by the human ego, in other words, ego gratification. And, the outcome will be self-defeating. Of this you can be most assured. For most definitely you will find that others will not respond or be as impressed as you envisioned they would be because of your exercising, for they will be far too self-absorbed in their own lives to take the time to focus on you, and you may just end up no longer even desiring the exercise that could have contributed to your well-being!

Now, we do not say this about others to say that their self-absorption would be bad or wrong, although if their approval is the motivation around your exercising, then you will most probably end up feeling they are bad or wrong for not noticing you as you would wish them to. We simply state that expecting others to be as absorbed in your affairs as you are would be expecting more than you will usually find. Even if that human is a parent, we would not encourage undertaking any activity for the sole purpose of pleasing or impressing another. It is the surest way to create disappointment in one's life. Ask yourself this: Do you spend your days observing what others are doing simply so you can comment on the marvelous things that others are doing? We doubt that you will answer in the affirmative. Nevertheless, humans who berate themselves for not being all that they should be are doing so because they truly believe someone may be watching and judging their performance. Interesting, isn't it? But do note, also, that when others do judge you, and that does occur, it is always in relation to how you are affecting the image they have of themselves and their fears regarding how others will perceive them. For example, let us say you have decided to tell a friend that the clothes that person wears are unacceptable to you. Would you be doing this in order to help this person feel better about who he or she is, or would it be because you are uncomfortable to be seen with this person, fearing others will judge your taste in clothes and friends? Now we do not bring up these situations to create bad feelings in you, it is simply to help you see the difference between thought forms that can enhance one's well-being, and thought forms that may be causing discomfort to you.

Another way of looking at the difference between thought forms is to consider that any thought form that separates you from others, such as "How are others looking at me?," will be a thought form that is helping you to have sad or unhappy thoughts. Conversely, any thought form that keeps your heart open to unconditional love of self or others, without judgment, is a thought form that is healing and creates well-being in oneself.

Humans are very capable of carrying both kinds of thought forms in great abundance -- and they may reside side by side. You know you have thoughts that make you very happy and create good feelings inside you at the same time as you are carrying thoughts that create discomfort within. What is interesting is that most humans wish only to be one way or another. If they have a few very uncomfortable thoughts, then they decide that their whole lives are terrible, and life is awful. They forget to remember the good thoughts as well. People wish to be linear in their thinking. However, we will tell you now, and forever:

The human mind is not linear. You think many different kinds of thoughts all the time. And you will find very often that you will have at least two different kinds of thoughts about the same thing. That is the true nature of the human mind. Give yourself permission to know this. It can be very, very useful information to know about oneself. And it will lead to self-love and forgiveness if you allow it!

Yes, beloved friend, understand that the human mind is much more complex than you have heretofore allowed yourself to accept.

So, now, we are looking for the thoughts that you wish to transform and release from the human mind so that you can carry more of the thoughts that will be healing and create well-being within. These are the thoughts that will literally change your mind and subsequently your whole being, if you will allow such. It can be done, beloved one; trust that this is so.

Let us say, then, that you have a thought form related again to the example of exercising. In this thought form you have become angry because others are not noticing and agreeing that your exercising has been quite a wonderful thing. You are finding now, that the original impetus for exercising is no longer there. The energy, so to speak, is being drained in regard to your continuing to pursue this endeavor. You are finding it more and more difficult to find the time and the energy necessary to undertake this exercising, and so you are becoming distressed, because somewhere inside you, you know that if you were to continue, it would be good for you.

You may find this particular set of circumstances regarding many, many different issues. This could be in regard to changing one's diet, ceasing the inhalation of cigarettes or ingestion of mind-altering substances, or any activity where you have decided that the opinions of others would govern your actions. Note, now, that there are conflicting thoughts regarding this issue, whichever one it is. You resent the response or lack thereof from the others about you, yet you still know, somewhere, that it would be good to start or continue a behavior that would enhance your well-being.

What to do? First it is most important to find a quiet time away from the din of other activities, where you can sort out your thoughts and note the accompanying feelings associated with these thoughts. This activity can be accomplished in many ways. You may simply sit quietly and open yourself to a healing, peaceful energy that will provide you with a comfortable space in which to do this work. Or you may find a trusted friend or counselor who would be willing to work with you to see what the thought forms are that you are carrying regarding a particular issue. Or you may wish to write down the thoughts that come to you, noting the feelings attached to each thought.

We again ask you please to keep yourself open to noting thoughts that may be diametrically opposed to one another. They may not make sense when you write them down and look at them. But we are asking you *not to judge*

22

what you find. Simply accept the thoughts and feelings. They are valid and they are part of who you are in this moment. We wish you to consider always *honoring all and everything of who you are in every moment.* You are becoming, growing, changing in every moment. That is the excitement and adventure of the human experience. *Love and enjoy it all!*

Now, let us assume you have discovered or listed the thought forms that are making you uncomfortable, sad, unhappy, or angry – for example: "Others do not appreciate my efforts. If I were better at what I try, then they would notice me. I will never be successful at anything I try. This is something I simply do not do well. I give up" -- and so on. All have had such thoughts. So, what can be done to ease the feelings that come with these thoughts?

First and foremost: Accept them and forgive yourself for feeling them. This is crucial. If you find yourself resisting the thoughts, they do not go away. It is Cosmic Law: *Whatever you resist will persist.* If you do not believe this is so, please, beloved one, test this for yourself. Whenever you have tried by any other means to "get rid of" or simply remove what you no longer want about yourself, you will note that the progress is slow and painful, or that there is simply no progress at all.

Do not condemn yourself for your thoughts and feelings. Please, respect what has gone into the making of these thought forms that you have carried for so long. They most probably have been with you for more than one lifetime, and in this lifetime you have finally decided you no longer wish to carry them. Bravo! But first, have compassion and love for self for all that has gone into creating who you are.

You are wonderful, unique, and changing constantly. Now you have decided to change some of your thoughts. And this is how it can be done:

Now that you are done condemning yourself, and have decided to simply accept everything about who you are, you can work to transform what you have carried for so long. First, we ask you to find a quiet, comfortable space. Be in solitude for this most important work. In this space we ask you to breathe in a healing radiance until it expands your diaphragm and fills your lungs completely. Breathe it in gently and lovingly. Allow it to love you and help heal your body. As you breathe this radiance in, whatever healing color it may be [violet, green, yellow, blue, or a golden-white are recommended], think again the thoughts, one at a time. As you think each thought, *see a luminescent violet Light permeating the thought.* Allow the Light to permeate the thought completely and then give the thought, in its transformed state of Light, away to the Light. Simply release each thought, one at a time, and let it go.

There may be feeling and emotion attached to each thought as you release it. Allow yourself to feel these feelings completely and fill yourself with the violet Light as you do this. Keep breathing the healing radiance all through the process. *Be patient!* Allow the process to unfold as it will. Give yourself permission to feel all you need to feel in regard to each thought form as you transform it with the violet Light and give it away to the Light.

You may wish to allow yourself to do this exercise more than once as you discover different layers and emotions attached to each thought form that you simply did not know you were carrying. Be kind, gentle, and patient with yourself as you go through this process, and remember to allow yourself time and space in which to continue the process as the feelings become known to you.

After each session of releasing into the violet Light the transformed thought forms, give yourself time to rest in a luminescent golden-white Light that will seal in the healing and replace the thought forms you have released with this benevolent radiance. Simply sit for a while, bathing in the golden-white Light. Some have called this the Light of the Christos or the Christ Light. What you wish to call it does not matter. But know that it is an all-forgiving Light that is here, available to all human beings to help them heal and release and be completely well again. And so, the process is done.

Chapter 5

Asking for Help

We congratulate you, beloved friend, on the work you have done so far! The desire to change how one has been and to open to new vistas of possibility of how one can be is a very brave and at times arduous task for most living upon the human plane. Yet you are allowing yourself to open to the possibility that this kind of change is possible. Indeed, you do accept that change is occurring all the time. At times you have not always been delighted with how that change has occurred for you and the others you see about you. The normal course of action for most humans is to seek "security" and resist change, for change becomes the unknowable.

You know how you have dealt with your uncomfortable life circumstances in the past; why would you want to learn how to deal with change and the new circumstances it will most certainly bring? And yet, every day you must do just that. *For every day there is change. Nothing ever stays the same. The adventure of living is to experience change and growth for greater self-awareness.*

The opportunity you are giving yourself now is, so to speak, to become the captain of your own fate instead of perceiving your world as a place where you must suffer through the vicissitudes of fate. Do you see the difference, beloved one? What you are doing is deciding to create your world instead of believing that it has been created for you, and that you must simply grin and bear it. Keep a stiff upper lip, so to speak.

Some of your religions will tell you that this kind of thinking is not to be countenanced, that God, or however Infinite Source is called, is a Master to be obeyed and is separate from who you are. But we will say this is simply not so.

What we will say instead, is that the Cosmic Laws are to be understood by you as a being of manifestation from Infinite Source, and part of that understanding is to accept that you create what occurs for you upon this human plane.

If you decide that you are a being subject to the whims of a punishing God, then that is what your world will be. And for many, this is the case.

If you decide that you are connected to, and a manifestation of, a Benevolent Source of Love and Light, and that you are here to extend that Love and Light to others, then that is what you will find in your world.

That is Cosmic Law, beloved friend, at its simplest interpretation: You will reap what you sow. If you sow the seeds of fear and mistrust in your world, then that is what you will experience.

Now, there will be many of you who will say, but Master, what of all the suffering and the many victims that we see in the world all around us? What of the little children who do not yet understand what the world is, who in their innocence and youth are slaughtered and made to suffer so?

27

How can they ever even know these Cosmic Laws when they are suffering before they could comprehend what the world could be for them?

And we will answer: For them, the world has been a cruel place, indeed -- as it has been for *everyone* at some time or another. This is a reality that one cannot avoid knowing about the Earth plane.

What we ask you to consider, however, is another reality. All who are on the Earth now have lived thousands of times before. Thousands of times. In the lives that are cut short, there are many more reasons than the human mind can comprehend for the cruelty one may witness. These beings who choose such a life have come in to balance past life experiences in such a manner. For many, it is to bring greater awareness to the whole human plane for the need to be compassionate and merciful. You do understand that many beings awaken to compassion when they see the young ones suffer. So, very often the young ones choose these shortened life spans in order to call others to their true natures.

Certainly, they will be balancing Karma from past embodiments, but it is not our business to evaluate or judge how that may have been created. All we need to know is that if we open to a greater awareness and become more compassionate and caring, then fewer beings will need to choose such embodiments in order to balance Karma in this manner.

Now, you will say, "But Master, it is fine and good to say these things. But how can these little ones even be aware that this is what they are choosing to do?" Again, this is an excellent question. Understand, beloved child, there is more to you than the eye can see. We have called you a direct manifestation from Infinite Source. And, as such, you carry many vibrational frequencies. In each one of these frequencies you will find a direct correlation with Source.

Even if your human mind cannot relate to and comprehend what is occurring around you for the sake of communication with others, it simply does not mean that you do not know. You do know, on some level, *even now*, why you have chosen the path and course of action you have taken to this point. As you awaken, you simply have a greater awareness of what you already know and have always known.

So, before these children embody and the veil of forgetfulness falls over them, they are aware that they will be making certain choices as to where they will be born, and how their lives will be before they ultimately awaken and remember.

Now, you are in a position to awaken and remember what you have always known. And we are here to be of service to you in this regard, if you will allow.

Who are we, and why would we wish to be of service to you? Perhaps you have been a person who has harmed another in this life, or have been told at some point of your life that you are not a very good or kind person, or perhaps you simply feel like that is true about yourself. If this is your belief, then you will probably also believe that you do not deserve help from anyone. Indeed, you may believe that you do not deserve *any* kind of grace or goodness to be a reality in your life.

If you feel this way, then you are not alone. All human beings have a history, in this life and in others. In the eyes of one who is inclined to judge, all have reasons to believe they are unworthy of a good life, unworthy of help of any kind, and deserving of every bit of suffering they are experiencing. If you decide that this is true for you, and you wish to continue on your path as you have always done, then we cannot help you, nor would we be willing to intervene.

You see, *the Earth is a plane of free will.* And, as such, you do create your reality without intervention from any of the other planes of existence, one of which is where we reside. This is why the Earth does indeed look so dark and hopeless to so many. We can watch you make your choices, but unless you ask directly for our help or the help of any other being of Light -- including the being you may call God, Allah, or Buddha and which we call Infinite Source -- then there is nothing we can do but watch and wait.

You see, beloved friend, *you are on this Earth to awaken and know that you are Light,* and that Creation is filled with beings of Light who exist simply to be of service to all Creation, yourself included. These beings do not judge you. They cannot. They are not of the Earth, where judgment was created. They are of the higher-vibrational frequencies that cannot even carry the vibrational frequency of judgment.

All are simply beings of Light, and that Light comes to you as Infinite Love. It is a kind of Love that you can experience while you are in a human body. It is a Love that will awaken you to your true nature, which is also this Love that never judges, and never asks anything in return but to be this Love. It exists simply to exist within you and allow you to open to expressing this to all and everything upon the human plane.

You carry this Love within you *now*. If you did not, you would cease to exist. It is the life force that sustains you. We are, from where we reside, in continual awe and gratitude for the power of this life force that is infinite, that is from Source. When you awaken and know it, you are free.

So, we exist to support this life force, and in so doing, to share this life force, this Love, with you and aid you to awakening to know that you are this life force, this Love, also. That is why we would never, in fact, could never judge you. It is impossible.

We ask you simply to consider that there is no need for you to continue to judge self. It only perpetuates your suffering and ultimately the suffering of the whole human plane. Let it go, beloved one, and as you let it go, then we can come to you. Simply ask and we are with you. We have been with you always, but when you ask, you can then *know* this to be true.

We are simply Beings of Light, as are you. We, however, have not chosen to be human at this time, but to be a link between you, in your human form, and Infinite Source. We are another resource, if you will, that can aid you in awakening to your own true nature. Simply call to us and we are with you. It does not matter what words you use to ask for our help. The intent behind the words is all that matters. If

31

you ask with an open heart and a conviction that we will aid you in any way possible, we are free to help and it is done.

However, you may be disappointed if you ask for our help in a way that to you would be a testing of whether we exist, or an experiment that if we give you what you want, then you know that we are real. You see, we are not here to answer whims of fancy or to help you create great wealth or fame. If that is your path, then such will come to you whether we intervene or not on your behalf. No, beloved friend, we are here to help you help yourself. We are here to help you awaken to your true nature as a being of Light who can then help light the way for all who dwell on Earth.

We do not have goals as you may have goals to accumulate things while you are on Earth. As the Master [Jesus] said, true riches will be found in heaven, by opening to the true, higher-vibrational nature of your being. When you awaken and know your Light within and how to live in peace and harmony within this Light as you walk the Earth, the need for possessions and approbation simply falls away. You know you have abundance. It is the true abundance of a rich, awakened being.

So, ask, beloved being. Ask, and you will see. Simply ask for help from the Light and the beings of Light to help you awaken and know your true self, and it will be known to you. Words will begin to come to you from your true self. Some have called your true self your Higher Self, your Totality, the entity that informs you. It does not matter what it is called. But as you ask to know, your life will begin to unfold in a way that it will be known to you. *It will be known to you.*

We can give you words to use to begin this process. These words are affirmations. These are ways of affirming that you are seeking your true nature so you can be whole and complete in the Light while you still walk the Earth.

Chapter 6

Creating Affirmations

Affirmations are words spoken with clarity and purpose that create healing, growth, and greater awareness of one's true self.

It is most important, dear one, to understand that these spoken words are not to be used to harm another, gain personal acclaim, or answer the needs of a greedy heart. A greedy heart is created when there is fear of lack. A heart that is awakening knows that all needs are answered in the abundance of Light that is for everyone.

It is the purity of thought, emotion, and inspiration that leads to the effectiveness of these spoken words. So, the question becomes, how does one know that these qualities are present in the affirmations one is creating? This is what we will share with you now:

The most important ingredient in creating powerful, healing affirmations is a quiet, centered meditative heart that is willing to listen to the inspiration of its own Totality in formulating the affirmations.

We ask you, then, beloved friend, to sit quietly in a place where you will not be disturbed by the life around you. We ask you to open to the Light, and allow it to fill your form. Then ask for help. Breathe in the healing radiance that comes to you very quietly and evenly as you sit in this silence. Allow yourself to sit in this way for a few moments. Just sit. Sit and ask that help and inspiration come to you. Whatever words come to you, write them down. Some will be confusing. Some will be nonsensical. This is fine. Some of the words will be your own human mind struggling to stay in control of the process, and this is fine. In time you will know the difference between the words coming from your Totality (or Higher Self) for your Highest Good, and the words coming from your mind, which wishes to stay in control of this process. The ultimate goal is simply to let go of the mind's creation and trust what comes to you from inspiration. Some suggested beginning affirmations to help with this process are:

- I AM open and listening to my Totality as it guides me in creating affirmations for my Highest Good.

- I Love my human mind and allow it to rest as I trust the words of inspiration that come from my Totality for my Highest Good.

- I sit easily and effortlessly in meditation with an open heart to hear my heart's desire for my Highest Good.

It is very powerful to use affirmations that begin with the expression: I AM. This acknowledges a connection to your Totality (or Higher Self), which is also called the I AM PRESENCE. It is also imperative that you continually express that that which you are affirming is *for the Highest Good*. When inspiration comes to you and you are not sure that it is for your Highest Good, ask if it is and be still and listen. You will know. An answer will come to you. You will feel it in your heart. And if it is not for your Highest Good, send the thought to Infinite Source for transformation and healing. Simply state: "I send this thought to Infinite Source for transformation and healing." Permeating the thought with violet Light as you say the affirmation enhances the effectiveness of this action.

Notice, beloved one, that all these affirmations are simple, positive statements. No negative words are used. All is loving and nurturing. Also, keep the affirmations in the present tense. You are stating that it is happening *now*, not in the future.

Some beings believe that is important to have "deadlines" as part of their affirmations and to be very specific about the outcome being sought. The human mind then becomes quite active in the process of creating such affirmations and the individuals often become disappointed when the outcome does not unfold as specifically decreed. By keeping all affirmations in the present tense, you automatically are leaving the opportunity open for the process to unfold.

It is important to trust your Totality to guide you in the creation of the affirmations. Allow your own guidance to show you that which is your heart's desire *without being limited by human thought.* The human mind desires specificity and the control of deadlines. The Light of Source does not need these things in order to co-create with your Totality upon the human plane.

Understand, dear one, that all affirmations open one to a *process.* With one's human mind, one simply does not

know the perfection of this process. One must simply trust --
and that becomes the biggest test of all. We encourage you to
develop patience with your affirmations and above all, to
trust that such will create an unfolding that will be in your
Highest Good.

Say your affirmations every day after you have
entered a meditative state and asked the Light to be with you.
As you do this, leave yourself open to inspiration for the
creation of new affirmations. Feel free to let go of
affirmations that no longer apply to where you are at that
moment. Understand, this is a process of unfolding and as
you change, your affirmations will change with you.

It is interesting to keep all your affirmations as you
grow into greater awareness to see where you have been and
how your awakening has created new awarenesses in you.
You will see how the healing of painful thought forms has
opened you up to grow and expand in new ways you never
dreamt might be possible.

This is, of course, what the experience will become
for you. You will begin to allow your true nature and all your
dreams to express through the power of these affirmations
into a creation in this reality. It will seem magical and
wonderful to you and you will radiate this awareness to those
about you who will see the change in you without a word
being spoken. Share what you are learning when others ask
you why you look and act so well. It can help others to heal
and become empowered themselves.

We will list some simple affirmations in the next
chapter that you may choose to use as you begin this process.

But we encourage you to remember to *sit each day in quiet meditation so that you can know the power of your own inspiration and how it can create change and healing in your life.*

Chapter 7

Suggested Affirmations

There are many, many different areas of one's life where affirmations can be applicable. We will only mention the areas we find are most often addressed. We suggest that you discover, in your moments of quiet and meditation, which areas are your focus at this time. As you discover the thought forms that you no longer wish to carry, this will become clear to you.

Obviously, the areas where you are feeling stress and any kind of difficulty will be the areas where there are thought forms that you wish to heal and transform, and then replace with affirmations that empower you to create for your Highest Good and that of the planet upon which you have chosen to reside at this time.

Remember, these affirmations are being created to help you understand and actualize your true nature as a fully empowered and co-creative being of Light who has chosen to be alive at this time. This is an essential awareness in creating these affirmations. These are "I" statements of positive intent. If you find your affirmations expressing a desire to change the world around you and the people in it, instead of working to create change within yourself, begin again from the center of your own being.

Begin with "I." Use the present tense. And remember, you are not alone. Beings of Light are eager to help you. Simply ask.

Please be aware that we use the word "Source" to designate the Creator of All and Everything. You may choose to call Source whatever you wish in using these affirmations. Simply replace the word "Source" wherever you see it with the name of a Being of Light that is more agreeable for you.

Affirmations for Health and Well-being:

- I accept the Healing Light of Source into my physical form.

- I AM healthy and well.

- I exercise and eat well to be healthy.

- I AM open to finding new, positive ways to maintain my health and well-being.

- I AM finding friends and support that aid me in maintaining my health and well-being.

- I release all negative karmic attachments within my physical form that limit my health and well-being.

- I ask for help from beings of Light on this and other planes in releasing these negative karmic attachments and aiding me in being healthy and well.

- I open to accept my healing.

- I AM in balance and harmony.

- My body is healthy, strong, and supple.

Affirmations for Soul Growth and Awakening:

- I AM accepting with full awareness the Light of Source as it fills my being, creating growth and awakening within me.

- I ask the beings of Light to aid me in awakening to full awareness of the Light of Source.

- I surrender to the Love and Light of Source and I allow it to be my guiding force.

- I AM finding friends who support my path of awakening and awareness of the Light of Source.

- I AM open to inspiration from Source in guiding me on my daily path.

- I AM the center and All is flowing to me in perfect order.

- I AM aware that all that I do is infused with the Love and Light of Source and I allow this energy full reign within my physical form.

- I take time each day to reflect and meditate. I understand that this allows me greater awareness of my empowering connection to Source.

- I ask for help from beings of Light on this and other planes in opening to even greater awareness and awakening of the Light of Source within me.

- I acknowledge my connection to the Light and Love of Source which is already within me. I am simply awakening to the awareness.

- I recognize and accept my path as it unfolds with ease.

- The Light from my heart infuses all my actions.

- All that I do in awakening to the awareness of Source is of the Highest Good.

- I trust my path. I trust the Light. I see that every experience is my opportunity to awaken to my true nature as a being of Light.

- I know that I AM Light and Love choosing a human experience.

- I AM the observer and the observed. I see with wisdom and compassion.

- I release all preconceived ideas of who I AM becoming.

- I release all judgment of self and others.

- I AM still and listen with an open and compassionate heart.

Affirmations for Healed Relationships:

- I share the Love and Light of Source easily within my relationships.

- I see my friends and family filled with the Love and Light of Source.

- I release all negative karmic bonds and am open to the Highest Good for this relationship.

- I ask for help from beings of Light on this and other planes in healing this relationship.

- I release all preconceived ideas of how this relationship must heal. I trust that the healing process, however it may be, will be for the Highest Good of All concerned.

- I release all judgment of self and others.

- I open in meditation to wisdom and compassion in healing this relationship.

- I release all fears of abandonment and understand that I AM within the Love and Light of Source in every moment.

- I release any need to control this relationship and turn over the relationship to the Love and Light of Source for healing.

Affirmations for Abundance and Prosperity:

- I recognize and accept the abundance of time and money to accomplish all that I AM inspired to do.

- I AM in the flow of the Love and Light of the Infinite Source.

- I give myself to Source to guide me in creating a vocation that is my true expression of the Light and Love of Source made manifest here and now.

- My heart sings as I earn my daily bread.

- I give myself to the inspiration of Source in all I do and Source responds in Abundance.

- I recognize and accept the abundance and prosperity in my life.

- All my needs are met by the Light and Love of Source.

- I trust the flow.

Affirmations for the Earth:

- I honor the Earth and am aligned with it for the healing of the whole planet.

- The Earth is filled with the healing Light and Love of Source.

- I accept and recognize the beauty and abundance of the Earth and offer myself as a caretaker of its abundance.

- I see the Earth as healed and whole.

- I invoke all beings of Light to continue to create the harmony and balance of all creation.

- I understand and accept that as I heal, the Earth heals and I invoke the beings of Light to help us all.

- I invoke the Archangels Gabriel, Raphael, Michael and Uriel to seal all spaces in Divine Pyramids of healing Light.

- I ask all Ascended Beings and Beings of Light to help us, all and everything, to be open, protected, and healed in the Light.

Please remember, dear one, as you use these and the other affirmations that you will create, to keep your heart and mind open to the process of healing that will be occurring as you say these words. *Intent is everything.* If you trust the power of your own words in creating healing and change within you, then *it shall be so*.

Personalize these words to encompass your world and your situation. Use the names of your friends and family. Place yourself in a space that allows you to open to the Light and Love of Source as it comes to you in response to your words. *Trust, beloved one, trust, and remember, you are never alone.* Accept the blessings of the Light and all the beings of Light. Allow us to work with you. Go in Peace.

St. Germain

Appendix A

Introduction to Psychoenergetic Healing

If you are interested in doing the work of personal transformation and healing suggested throughout this book, you may be interested in an innovative healing modality which I (Martin) have come to call *Psychoenergetic Healing.*

As a clinical psychologist trained extensively within the traditional paradigm of psychology and psychotherapy, I found myself increasingly dissatisfied. As I began to open to the Light I also began to search for better ways to do my work.

Searching for Better Ways: Can you imagine the practice of medicine before the invention of X-ray machines or microscopes? Would you want to refer someone to a doctor who refuses to consider anything that is not visible to the naked eye? The field of psychotherapy, as it is taught in graduate school today, can be likened to the practice of medicine based on a 19th-century view of the world. While there are many fine traditionally-trained psychotherapists out there, psychotherapy is still very much a "hit or miss" endeavor. We propose that the practice of psychotherapy (and healing in general) cannot advance significantly without a "shift in paradigm," i.e., a fundamental reorientation.

Psychoenergetic Healing is based on a "new" paradigm that is compatible with ancient wisdom teachings as well as modern sciences. Cutting-edge physicists have now come to similar insights as ancient mystics: All there is, all matter and all of Creation, is "patterned" energy, vibrating to specific frequencies which distinguish one manifestation of energy from another.

What is Psychoenergetic Healing? All psychological manifestations, such as thoughts, feelings, and behavior patterns, are likewise "patterned" energy. Effective psychological healing, regardless of the method or technique, occurs when there is a change in the basic energies that charge our feelings, thoughts, memories, and habits. While all psychotherapeutic methods are intended to produce such healing, most do not target the energetic level directly.

Psychoenergetic Healing takes into account that human beings are not only physical, emotional, and mental beings but most essentially also spiritual beings. This truth is not a mere statement of faith; it can be experienced in a direct, tangible manner. No matter what names or interpretations we prefer, a spiritual, healing energy or Light can be accessed by all human beings regardless of our belief systems and can be utilized effectively for healing on all levels. This is an important step beyond physical, emotional, or mental approaches to healing, as the spiritual energies are the "highest" and most powerful energies available.

The practitioner of Psychoenergetic Healing utilizes a variety of techniques which affect the mental and emotional energies on a fundamental level, thus going directly to the source of one's discomfort. While going to the core of the matter may be a scary thought to many, it is actually a very healing, safe, efficient, and effective method which does *not* require the unbuffered reliving of traumatic memories or painful feelings.

What Happens in a Typical Session? What happens in a session is very much guided by the individual's needs and issues, making each session a unique experience. Most sessions include elements of traditional "talking therapy" expanded upon with work in "inner space" where clients can perceive and experience the richness of their inner world. Facilitated by the therapist, the client achieves a heightened state of consciousness in which he or she may become aware of physical sensations, colors, images, thoughts, feelings or other perceptions (including, for instance, images of past lives).

While each client has a different experience, all are able to perceive the flow of energies within. These inner perceptions then guide the course of the healing work. Using what could be called a "psychological X-ray technique," the client can become aware of the core issue and then observe the process of healing on an energetic level as it is occurring. Although getting in touch with painful feelings or experiences may cause some temporary discomfort, a tangible shift and relief can often be felt within minutes. Because the client has control over his or her "inner space" and all therapeutic interventions are guided by the client's inner perceptions, this approach to healing is experienced as empowering and safe.

Who Can Benefit From Psychoenergetic Healing? Most of us are not consciously aware of the subtle energies that fuel our behaviors and states of mind at all times, and yet, we all have noticed emotional energies in action, such as when we experience intense anger, fear, or resentment. If we do not release and balance negative energies properly, but instead "sweep them under the rug," they may linger in our emotional body for an unlimited time, causing further disturbance. They may even manifest in physical disease. To gain or maintain a state of harmony and health it is essential to attend to these energies, i.e., to resolve inner conflicts, release traumatic memories, and heal emotional issues.

Our experience has shown that Psychoenergetic Healing can be an effective approach regardless of the presenting problem, as all thoughts, memories, feelings, and habits exist as "patterned" energies and can be treated as such. Psychoenergetic Healing has been successfully applied to a wide variety of issues, including anger, fear, depression, addictions, sexual issues, co-dependency, low self-esteem, traumatic experiences, psychosomatic illnesses, pain, grieving and loss, etc. Clients of all ages, including children and adolescents, have benefited greatly from Psychoenergetic Healing, regardless of their belief systems or prior experience with energy-based healing. A sizable number of our clients have already done a significant amount of inner work, be it emotional or spiritual in nature, and desire to further their growth by addressing those issues which previously seemed intractable. Thus, to benefit from Psychoenergetic Healing, a commitment to growth is more relevant than the nature of the problem, or whether it fits into any traditional diagnostic pigeon-hole.

Appendix B

Books by the Authors

Balancing the Light Within: *A Discourse on Healing from the Ascended Master St. Germain,* by Linda Stein-Luthke and Martin F. Luthke, ISBN 0-9656927-0-1, 54 pp., US $6.95. This is the first in a series of channeled discourses from the Ascended Master St. Germain. It discusses the nature of Light and love, useful tools of awareness, the body's chakras and their colors, as well as how to heal self and others with metaphysical means. This slender book is a great introductory text for readers without much prior exposure to the topics of healing, the human energy body, and how to use the Light in a conscious and beneficial manner. Many of our clients have read the text repeatedly.

Affirmations and Thought Forms: *You Can Change Your Mind! A Discourse from the Ascended Master St. Germain,* by Linda Stein-Luthke and Martin F. Luthke, ISBN 978-0-9656927-1-X, 60 pp., US $6.95. A channeled discourse on the use of affirmations and the power of thought forms and how to use both for healing purposes, with an emphasis on self-empowerment and self-awareness.

Angels and Other Beings of Light: *A Discourse from the Ascended Master St. Germain,* by Linda Stein-Luthke and Martin F. Luthke, ISBN 0-9656927-3-6, 84 pp., US $8.95. This book discusses the concepts of angels, Archangels,

Ascended Masters, twin flame, soul mates, and other beings of Light. The Master explains who they are, what their purpose is, as well as how to contact the beings of Light and actively work with them. In addition, you will learn how to experience your Higher Self. This popular book is a concise introduction into the realm of beings of Light and how you can benefit from their help.

Navigating the Fourth Dimension: *A Discourse from the Ascended Masters St. Germain and El Morya Khan,* by Linda Stein-Luthke and Martin F. Luthke, ISBN 0-9656927-5-2, 134 pp., US $11.95. This publication explains that humanity has the opportunity now to break free from the confines of the third dimension and to embrace the reality of the fourth dimension and beyond. We define the fourth dimension as a higher-vibrational state of being that is characterized by trust, empowerment, abundance, peace, balance, and harmony. It is based on the realization that we are beings of Light, who carry formidable power as co-creators of our universe. Living in the fourth dimension requires a conscious shift from relying on the fear-based ego mind to trusting the heart-centered guidance of our Higher Selves. The Ascended Masters discuss how to let go of our history, how to heal anger, fear and pain, and how to develop a personal knowing of our Light. Each one of us can now choose to live in a new paradigm -- the fourth dimension. The appendix contains the first ten issues of the Ascended Masters Newsletter.

Dispelling the Illusions of Aging and Dying*: A Discourse from the Ascended Master St. Germain,* by Linda

Stein-Luthke & Martin F. Luthke, Ph.D.; ISBN 0-9656927-6-0; 90 pp., US $11.95. In this book St. Germain discusses the two most basic fears that human beings possess -- the fears of aging and dying -- and how those very fears hold human beings in the grip of the process of aging and dying. The Master explains how to set yourself free from such fears and to see them for what they really are: illusions. The appendix contains seven issues of the Ascended Masters Newsletter.

Beyond Psychotherapy: Introduction to Psycho-energetic Healing, by Martin F. Luthke and Linda Stein-Luthke, ISBN 0-9656927-4-4, 228 pp., US $19.95. This is a fundamental text that describes in detail the healing approach that we developed over the years with the guidance of the Ascended Masters. *Beyond Psychotherapy* shows you how to work effectively with healing energies to heal body, mind, and spirit; past life trauma; anxiety; anger; addictions; depression; pain and other physical complaints; relationship issues; remote or recent traumatic experiences; and many other issues. You will learn about the theoretical foundations of energy healing, specific techniques and applications, and the risks and benefits of becoming a healer. Clearly and concisely written, *Beyond Psychotherapy* offers profound and practical information for anyone interested in energy-based healing methods. This book also is the textbook for students of Psychoenergetic Healing.

Riding the Tide of Change: Preparing for Personal & Planetary Transformation, by Martin F. Luthke, ISBN 0-9656927-2-8, 108 pp., US $9.95. This is a book on Earth changes from a metaphysical perspective. It emphasizes releasing fears, healing self, and understanding our role as co-creators during this time of transformation. The appendix contains suggested readings as well as information on practical preparedness.

How to Contact the Authors
Linda and Martin welcome your comments or questions and are available for workshops, seminars, and individual sessions (also by phone). Please contact us at 440-564-1496 or write to expansion@u-r-light.com.

Free Ascended Masters Newsletter
Please consider subscribing to a free e-newsletter with channeled material from the Ascended Masters as well as information about new books or workshops. Please send a blank e-mail to newsletter-subscribe@u-r-light.com or visit the Archives at www.u-r-light.com for past issues.

Order Information

• **On-line orders**: For more information, excerpts, and secure on-line orders (Visa/MC and Paypal accepted), please visit *www.u-r-light.com*. You may e-mail any inquiries to *expansion@u-r-light.com*. Please contact us for resale or quantity discounts.

• **Mail-in orders**: Please send your order -- including your e-mail address, if available -- to: Expansion Publishing, P.O. Box 516, Chagrin Falls, OH 44022, USA. We gladly accept credit cards (with name, number, expiration date), US-checks, or money orders.

• **Shipping for domestic orders**: Please add $2.00 for orders totaling up to $10, $3.00 for orders between $10 and $20, and $4.00 for orders over $20.

• **Shipping for international orders**: Please add $4.00 for orders totaling up to $10; $5.00 for orders between $10 and $20; and $6.00 for orders over $20.

• **Bookstores**: All titles are also available through your local bookstore. However, you may need to special-order them.

• **Phone orders**: Please call **Expansion Publishing** (888-240-2822) for credit card orders.